D0710319

My Life as a Pioneer

Ann H. Matzke

rourkeeducationalmedia.com

Teacher Notes available at
rem4teachers.com

www.rourkeeducationalmedia.com

PHOTO CREDITS: All Images Courtesy of North Wind Picture Archives: www.northwindpictures.com

Edited by: Precious McKenzie
Cover design by: Tara Raymo
Interior design by: Renee Brady

Library of Congress EPCN Data

My Life as a Pioneer/Ann H. Matzke
(Little World Social Studies)
ISBN 978-1-61810-147-1 (hard cover)(alk. paper)
ISBN 978-1-61810-280-5 (soft cover)
Library of Congress Control Number: 2011945874

Rourke Educational Media
Printed in the United States of America,
North Mankato, Minnesota

rourkeeducationalmedia.com
customerservice@rourkeeducationalmedia.com • PO Box 643328 Vero Beach, Florida 32964

Wagons Ho, **pioneers**! We say goodbye to friends and journey west to find a new home.

At Independence, Missouri, we join the **overland trail**.

Pioneer Fact

Towns near the start of the trail were called jumping-off places where pioneers bought wagons and supplies for the journey.

We pack our supplies into a covered wagon called a **prairie schooner**. Four oxen pull our wagon.

With no room to ride inside the wagon, we walk along the trail ten to twenty miles (16.903 – 32.186 km) a day.

PIONEER FACT

It was a 2,000-mile (3,220 kilometer) journey across the United States and took five to six months to complete.

We see new animals along the trail, like **buffalo**. **Native Americans** sometimes help on our journey.

We travel all day. At sunset we stop to unpack the wagon, fetch water, and gather wood for a campfire.

After supper there is fiddle music, games, and stories to tell before we make our beds and fall asleep.

Bad weather, accidents, or illness can stop a wagon for days.

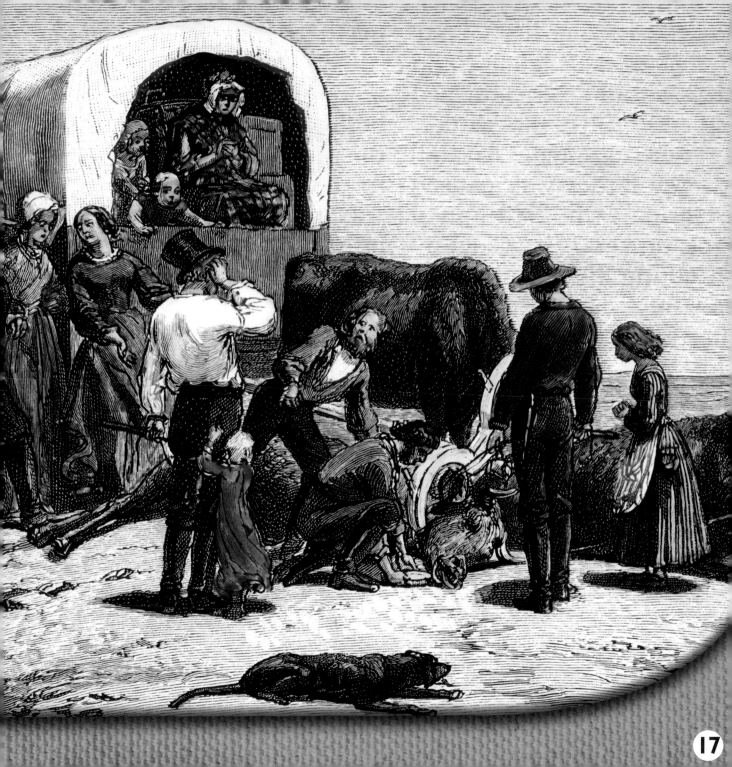

Landmarks guide our way.

After many hard months on the trail, we reach a new land ready to start a new life.

Picture Glossary

 **buffalo** (BUHF-uh-loh): An animal with thick fur and heavy horns, also called bison, that roamed the Great Plains in large herds.

 **landmarks** (LAND-marks): Objects in a landscape that can be seen from far away used to guide travelers.

 **Native Americans** (NAY-tiv uh-MER-uh-kuhns): The original people who lived in North America.

overland trail (oh-vur-LAND TRAYL): Pioneers followed paths westward known as the Oregon, California, and Mormon Trails.

pioneers (Pye-uh-NEERZ): The people who are the first to move and settle in unknown territory.

prairie schooner (PRAIR-ee SKOO-nur): A large, flatbed wagon that has a waterproof white canvas covering.

Index

buffalo   10

Chimney Rock   18

covered wagon   6

journey   3, 5, 8

supplies   5, 6

trail   4, 5, 8, 10, 20

Websites

www.nps.gov/oreg/historyculture/index.htm

www.historyglobe.com

www.indepmo.org/nftm/

About the Author

Ann H. Matzke is a children's librarian. She has an MFA in Writing for Children and Young Adults from Hamline University. Ann lives with her family near the Oregon and Mormon Trails in Gothenburg, Nebraska. She enjoys reading and writing books for children.

Ask The Author!
www.rem4students.com